# BANGS AND TWANGS
## SCIENCE FUN WITH SOUND

## VICKI COBB
## ILLUSTRATED BY STEVE HAEFELE

THE MILLBROOK PRESS
BROOKFIELD, CONNECTICUT

For Lexie Nicole Cobb
—Vicki Cobb

For Matt and Mitch, my little "Igors"
—S. H.

Published by The Millbrook Press, Inc.
2 Old New Milford Road
Brookfield, CT 06804
www.millbrookpress.com

Library of Congress Cataloging-in-Publication Data
Cobb, Vicki.
Bangs and twangs : science fun with sound / Vicki Cobb ; illustrated by Steve Haefele.
p. cm.
Summary: Text and simple experiments introduce sound, how it is carried through the air and
through objects, and how we hear it.
ISBN 0-7613-1571-3 (lib. bdg.)
1. Sound—Juvenile literature.  2. Sound—Experiments—Juvenile literature.  [1. Sound—Experiments.
2. Experiments.]  I. Haefele, Steve, ill.  II. Title.
QC225.5 .C63 2000
534'.078—dc21   00-022116

# 1   BANG IT AND TWANG IT

How many ways can you make sounds with your body without using your voice? Experiment and find out.

**REMEMBER, NOT ALL SOUNDS ARE POLITE.**

Cluck your tongue. Smack your lips. Make a kissing sound. Whistle. Sniff. Blow to make your lips flap. Clap your hands. Snap your fingers. Slap your thigh. Stamp your feet.

Now go around your house making different noises. The most obvious way to make sounds is to strike things. Bang pots and pans. Gently tap a glass with a spoon. Knock on wood. Pluck a guitar or a piano string or a stretched rubber band. Blow across the open top of a soda bottle. Listen to each sound you make. Is it like a musical note or is it an ordinary

The sound waves are traveling through air.

noise? Is it high or low? Can you match the tone with your voice? Hit something solid like a countertop. Hit something hollow like a box. Knock on a wall in several places. Some areas may sound hollow, some may sound solid. The solid sound comes from places where there is a beam or stud behind the wall.

The sound waves are traveling through wood.

A rubber band can show you what happens when a sound is made. First, hook a rubber band over a doorknob and stretch it tightly. Pluck it to create a sound. Look at it closely as it gives off its twang. Use a magnifying glass if you have one. You can see that the rubber band

STRETCH

moves back and forth very quickly. This kind of motion is called a vibration. Now pull the rubber band tighter. Pluck it again. Is the sound lower or higher? Are the vibrations faster or slower? The highness or lowness of a sound is called its pitch. The faster the vibrations the higher the pitch.

THICKER INSTRUMENT STRINGS HAVE A LOWER PITCH BECAUSE THEY VIBRATE SLOWER THAN THINNER STRINGS. WHEN YOU PRESS A STRING AGAINST THE FINGERBOARD, YOU SHORTEN IT TO MAKE AN EVEN HIGHER PITCH.

I AM TOO COOL!

THE PITCH OF A VIOLIN STRING ALSO CHANGES WHEN YOU PRESS IT AGAINST THE FINGERBOARD. A VIOLIN BOW DRAWN ACROSS A STRING MAKES IT VIBRATE FOR A LONGER TIME.

When you use your voice, you create vibrations. Make a humming noise and put your hand on your throat. Feel the vibrations of your voice box. Hum a high note and then a low note. Feel the difference.

**WHEN AIR PASSES THROUGH YOUR VOICE BOX IT MAKES TWO FLAPS OF SKIN VIBRATE.**

A vibrating object is only the beginning of a sound. You hear a sound because the air carries the vibrations to your ear. If there were no air, you would not hear the sound. The vibrations would be in a vacuum.

Want to "see" a sound? Talk to someone through dental floss? Make bangs and twangs that will entertain your friends and annoy your neighbors? Read on!

# 2  SEEING SOUND

You can use sound to make grains of sugar dance.

**HERE IS WHAT YOU NEED:**

a plastic bowl

Saran Wrap® (other plastic cling wraps don't work as well)

granulated sugar

a pot and a spoon

a rubber band

POP!

13

Stretch the plastic wrap over the bowl to make a smooth, airtight drum.

The wrap should cling to the bowl, but use a rubber band to hold it in place more securely.

Sprinkle about half a teaspoon of sugar on the wrap.

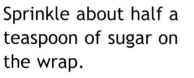

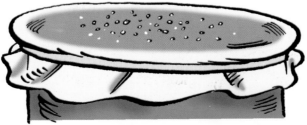

Hold the pot a few inches over your "drum" and bang the pot with the spoon. What happens if you move the pot off to the side? Will the sugar grains still jump? Watch the sugar jump with every sound you make. Now lean over the drum and sing a note. Do the sugar grains move? Try other noisemakers around your house to see how different sounds make the sugar move.

Here's what's happening. Air is made up of countless millions of tiny particles, called molecules, which are too small to see. When the pot vibrates, the air molecules surrounding it move. The air molecules bump into other air molecules farther away, setting them in motion. In this way, the vibration travels from one group of molecules to the next, like a wave. In fact, it is called a sound wave. When the sound wave reaches the stretched plastic wrap, the wrap vibrates the way the pot vibrates. The moving grains of sugar show the vibrations. Save this bowl for another experiment on page 20.

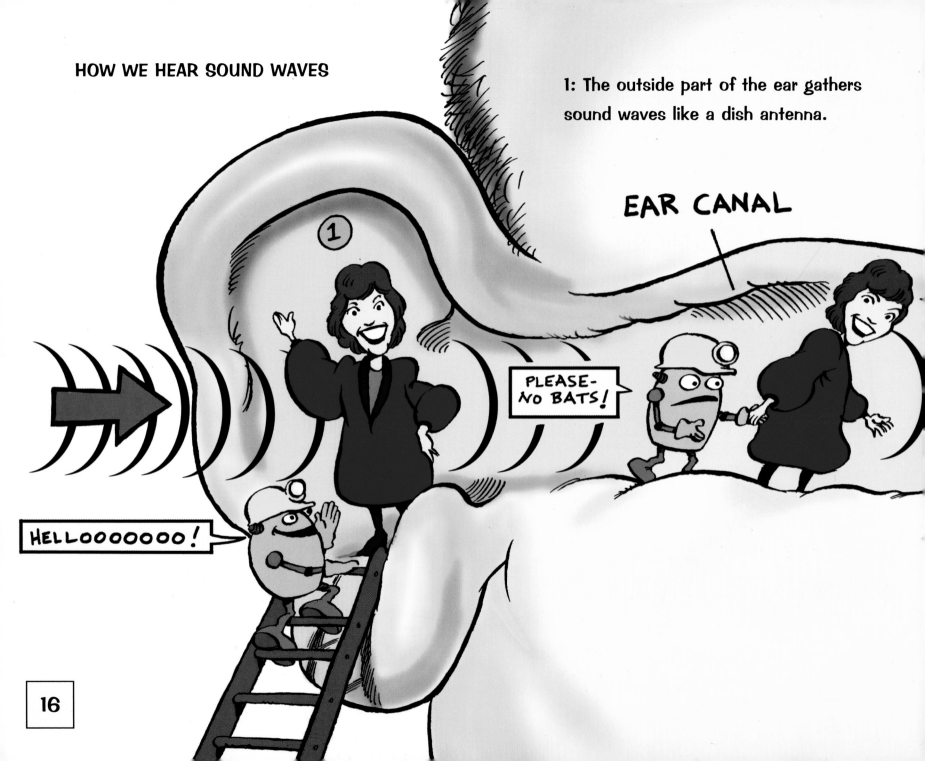

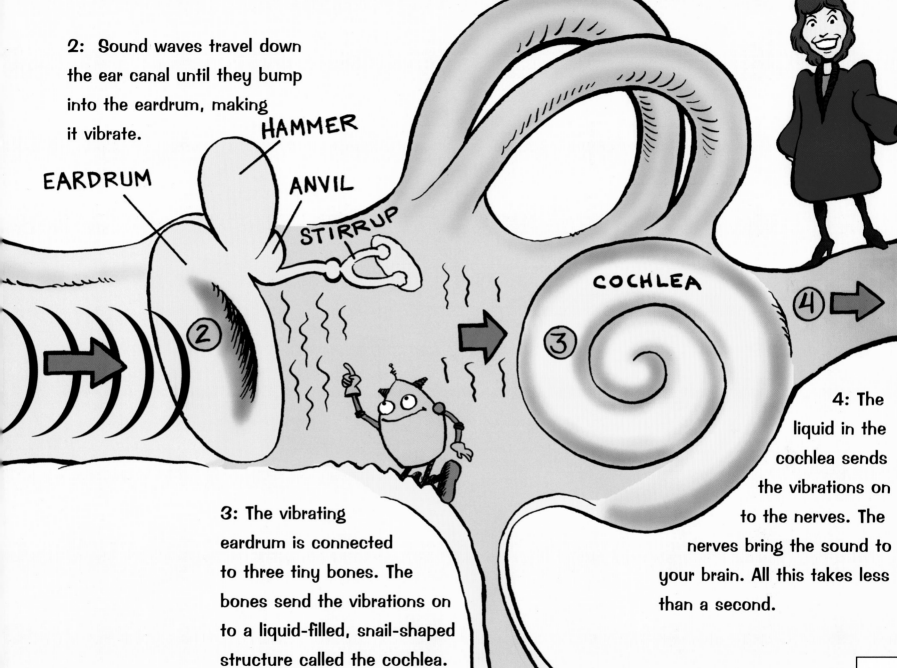

**2:** Sound waves travel down the ear canal until they bump into the eardrum, making it vibrate.

EARDRUM

HAMMER

ANVIL

STIRRUP

COCHLEA

**3:** The vibrating eardrum is connected to three tiny bones. The bones send the vibrations on to a liquid-filled, snail-shaped structure called the cochlea.

**4:** The liquid in the cochlea sends the vibrations on to the nerves. The nerves bring the sound to your brain. All this takes less than a second.

17

Vibrations are the reason your voice can travel through the telephone. The holes in the mouthpiece let vibrations from your voice reach a thin sheet of metal called a diaphragm. On the other side of the diaphragm is a container filled with grains of carbon. The vibrations of the diaphragm make the grains of carbon vibrate like the grains of sugar on the plastic wrap. Vibrating carbon grains give off electrical signals that are carried through

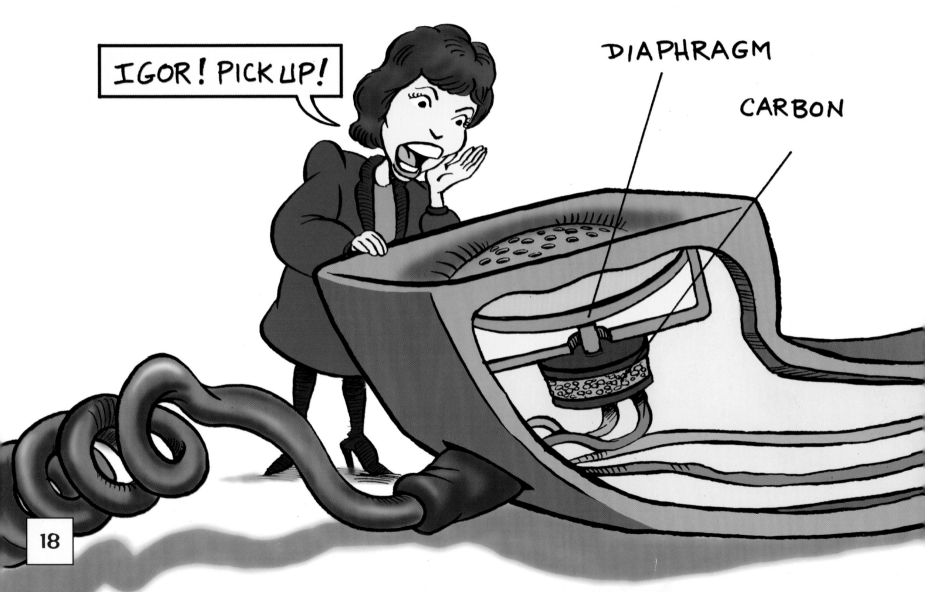

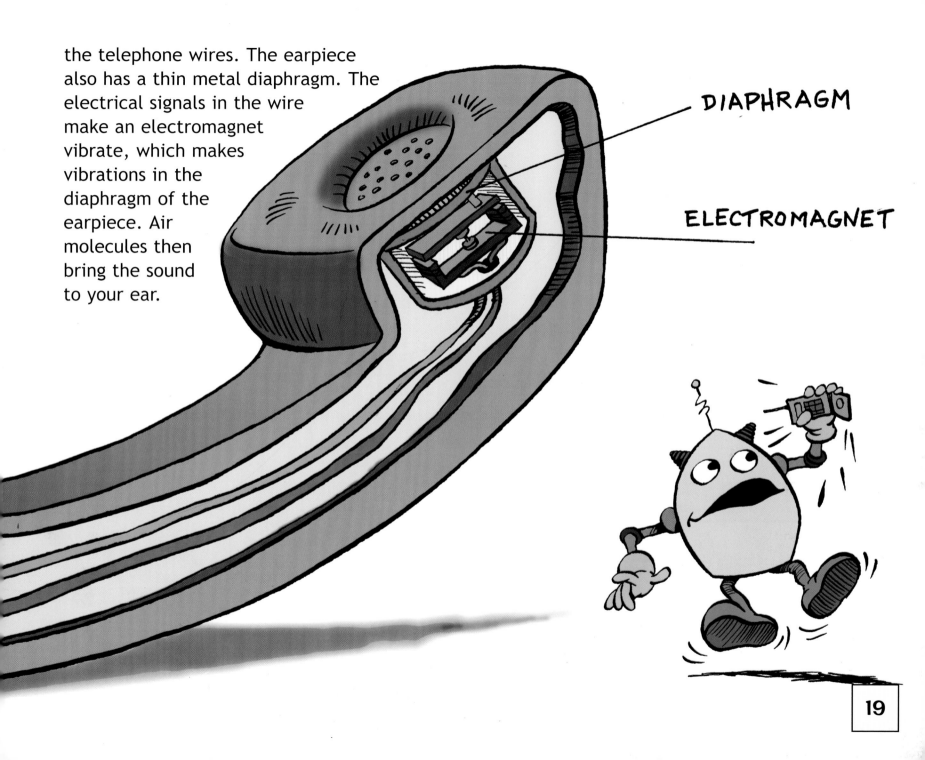

the telephone wires. The earpiece also has a thin metal diaphragm. The electrical signals in the wire make an electromagnet vibrate, which makes vibrations in the diaphragm of the earpiece. Air molecules then bring the sound to your ear.

DIAPHRAGM

ELECTROMAGNET

The pitch of a sound is caused by the rate of vibration or the number of vibrations per second. This is called the frequency. A musical note is a simple sound with one main frequency. Objects vibrate at their natural frequencies when struck. Most objects make a noise with many frequencies because different parts vibrate at different rates. You can detect the natural frequency of the plastic wrap on your sugar-coated bowl. Place the bowl on a piano and play a scale. Watch the grains of sugar. The grains will vibrate more when you hit the note that is the natural frequency of the stretched plastic.

WHEN AN OPERA SINGER HITS A NOTE THAT IS THE NATURAL FREQUENCY OF A WINE GLASS, IT CAN VIBRATE SO HARD THAT IT SHATTERS.

# 3  SCREECHERS

You can use moving air to make something vibrate and create a sound. Have you ever made a screech by blowing on a blade of grass? First, lay the grass flat along the side of one thumb and hold it tightly with the side of the other thumb. Then blow through the space between your thumbs. The grass vibrates, giving off a screeching sound.

You don't need a blade of grass to make a screecher. You can use paper, plastic wrap, or even cellophane tape. Cut a strip that is about 3 inches (8 centimeters) long and 1/4 inch (.6 centimeter) wide. Hold it flat between your thumbs and blow. Experiment with screechers made of different kinds of materials. Try: cellophane from an envelope window,  plastic "sleeves" around film negatives, foil from a gum wrapper.

$\frac{1}{4}$"

3"

You can make a screecher from a plastic drinking straw. Flatten one end of the straw. Cut the sides of the straw, as shown in the picture.

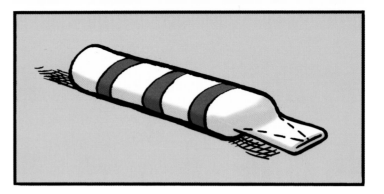

Put your mouth over the cut end of the straw. Gently squeeze the flaps together with your lips or teeth, and blow. When you are successful, you'll feel the flaps of the straw between your lips vibrate. You don't have to blow hard, but you may have to put your mouth in different places until you get the feel of it.

The vibrating straw makes the air inside the straw vibrate. The pitch depends on how long the straw is. See for yourself. Snip off an inch at a time, and notice how the pitch changes.

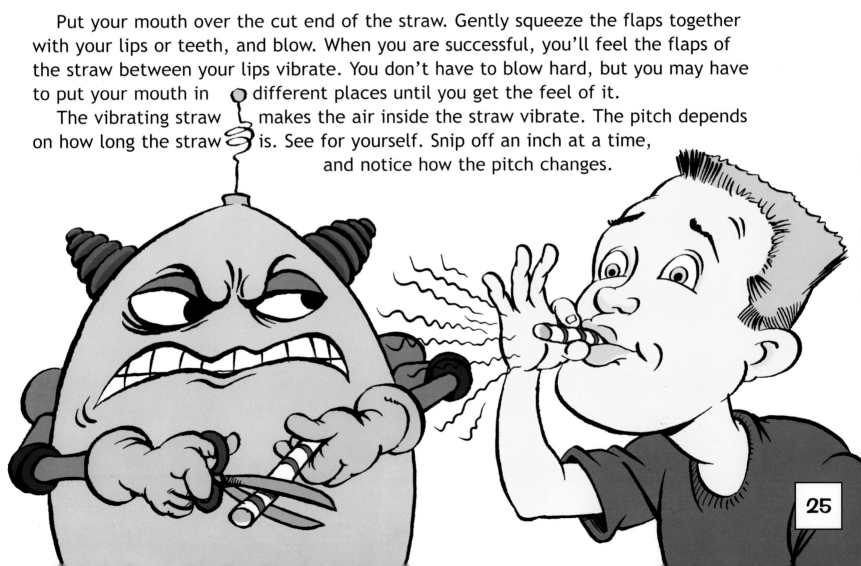

AN OBOE AND A CLARINET ARE MUSICAL INSTRUMENTS THAT USE VIBRATING PIECES CALLED REEDS.

REED

AIR HOLE TO CHANGE PITCH

WHEN THE MUSICIAN BLOWS INTO THE MOUTHPIECE, THE VIBRATING REED MAKES THE AIR IN THE INSTRUMENT VIBRATE. THE MUSICIAN CHANGES THE PITCH BY OPENING AND CLOSING VALVES, WHICH CHANGE THE LENGTH OF THE AIR COLUMN. IT TAKES SKILL TO MAKE A REED VIBRATE AND TO WORK THE VALVES.

BLOW THE STRAW AGAIN, IGOR. PUH-LEEZE ... BLOW THE STRAW, PLAY THE VIOLIN, ANYTHING!

The sound from a vibrating object travels in all directions. The outer ears of animals and people "gather" the sound waves and funnel them into the ear. Most bats have very large outer ears because they depend on collecting echoes as a kind of sonar. This means that a bat sends out high-pitched squeaks, which then bounce off an object and return to the bat's ears. Large ears collect sound better than small ones. Experiment and find out.

IT FEELS LIKE ALL THE BLOOD IS RUSHING TO MY BRAIN—IF I HAD ONE!

Here's something you can try with a friend. Have him or her whisper a message behind your back from across a room. Can you hear it? Now cup your hands backward to gather the sound behind you. Your cupped hands should make it possible to hear the whisper.

YOU CAN PERMANENTLY INJURE YOUR HEARING IF YOU LISTEN TO SOUNDS THAT ARE TOO LOUD.

31

You can improve your hearing immensely with "super ears."

**HERE IS WHAT YOU NEED:**

two paper cups
a pair of scissors

THIS PART HOOKS BEHIND EAR

Cut holes as shown in the bottom of the paper cups. Leave a small piece of the bottom to hook behind your ears. Put one cup over each ear. You now have super ears!

You can make super ears work even better if you cut an angled scoop out of the top. The super ears collect more sound waves and funnel them into your ears.

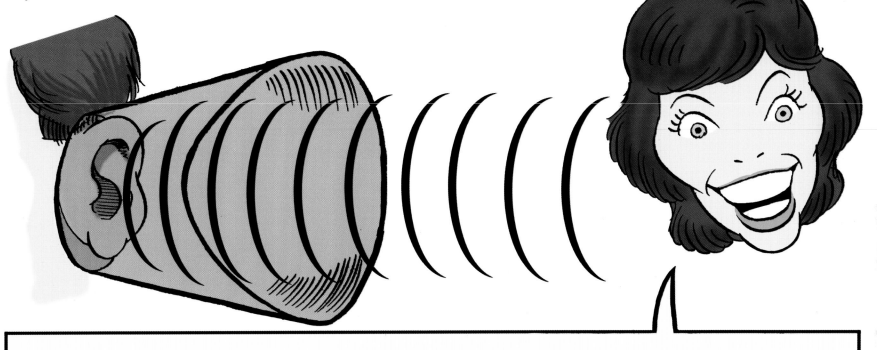

THIS SHAPE CAN WORK TO MAKE YOUR VOICE SOUND LOUDER. CUP YOUR HANDS AROUND YOUR MOUTH TO GATHER THE SOUND OF YOUR VOICE AND AIM IT.

# 5 PAPER CUP SPEAKER SYSTEM

You can use a paper cup to replace the amplifier and speakers of your stereo. Of course, the sound quality will be poor, but it's a fun experiment.

**HERE IS WHAT YOU NEED:**

scissors

a sharp straight pin

a record (it will get ruined—pick one up at a garage sale)

**I NEED A ROBOTOMY**

O

*The Artist Known As IGOR*

a paper cup

an old-fashioned turntable

Trim the paper cup so it is about half as tall. This allows you to reach inside and stick the pin halfway through the bottom. Put the record on the turntable. Turn it on at the proper speed for the record. Hold the cup so that the needle rests on the moving record. The cup should be held lightly and gently to pick up the sound from the record.

The cup and pin are not as good at picking up the music as a stereo system. But it is good enough to get some idea of the recorded sound. The first record players worked the same way as the needle and cup. They were just a lot bigger.

THESE LITTLE GROOVES IN THE RECORD MAKE THE NEEDLE VIBRATE FROM SIDE TO SIDE AS THE RECORD TURNS. THE VIBRATIONS GO FROM THE NEEDLE TO THE PICKUP ARM, WHERE THEY BECOME ELECTRICAL SIGNALS. WHEN THE SIGNALS ARE AMPLIFIED, OR MADE LOUDER, YOU HEAR THESE VIBRATIONS AS MUSIC.

So far, all the sounds you've made from this book travel through the air. But sound can travel through other things until it reaches the air and your ears. All it needs is molecules to travel through, whether they are air, water, wood, or some other kind of matter. Here are a few examples of devices that make sound travel:

YIKES!

CHILL OUT, IGOR. YOU'RE COMING IN LOUD AND CLEAR!

Would you believe that you can send your voice through dental floss? Do this experiment and see how.

**HERE IS WHAT YOU NEED:**

two heavy-duty cups
(for hot beverages)

a pushpin or safety pin

waxed dental floss
(tape variety)

a willing friend

YOUR EYES ARE LIKE DEEP POOLS OF DIESEL FUEL!

First, make a hole in the bottom of each cup with the pin.

Cut a piece of dental floss that is at least 15 feet (4.5 meters) long.

Thread an end of the floss into each cup. Make a big fat knot in the floss to keep it from slipping through the hole. You can also tape the floss in place.

In order for your squawky walkie-talkie to work, the floss must be stretched out straight. If you do this experiment outside, you can use 50 feet (15 meters) of floss or even more. If you do this inside, the dental floss will have to be no longer than the length of the longest room or hallway in your house.

To use the walkie-talkie, one person speaks into the cup while the other listens at the other end. When you want to switch, the speaker says, "Over."

SORRY-WRONG NUMBER

Here's the path of the vibrations:

1: First your voice sets air in motion. Voice vibrations cause the bottom of the cup to vibrate like a diaphragm. 2: The cup bottom makes the tight dental floss vibrate along its entire length. 3: These vibrations make the bottom of the other cup vibrate. 4: This makes the air vibrate, and your friend's ear hears sound at the other end. Since the vibrations are made by your voice, the sounds your friend hears are your words.

Your walkie-talkie is also a great squawker. With your thumb and index finger, grasp the dental floss next to the bottom of the cup. Lightly and quickly move your fingers along the floss as far as your arm reaches. A loud squawk should come out of the cup. Keep trying until you get a squawky walkie-talkie. This works because the wax on the dental floss makes your fingers stick briefly as they slip. As your fingers stick and slip along the floss, they set up vibrations. The cup bottom picks up the vibrations and magnifies them into a magnificent squawk.

# 7  SOUND EFFECTS

All the sounds you hear are combinations of different pitches, rhythms, and loudness. A sound effect is sound that is produced to imitate something else. Here are some sound effects you can make:

Put a small handful of rice in a metal pan. Now hold the pan flat and move it in a circle. It sounds like rain on a tin roof.

Another way to produce this effect is to pour a box of rice on a Ping-Pong® ball. Spread a large piece of cloth on the floor to catch the rice so you can use it again.

Pull a silk or polyester scarf back and forth across the back of a sofa cushion. Practice until you get a "swish" that sounds like the wind.

Put about a cup of dried beans or peas in a vinyl suitcase. Close the case. Tilt the ends of the suitcase up and down. As the peas move from side to side, you'll hear the sound of waves crashing on the beach. Another seashore sound is heard when you put a seashell to your ear.  The shell collects sound from the air around your ear. The sound echoes inside the shell. The echoes sound like waves at the seashore.

Blow across the top of an empty soda bottle to imitate the sound of a foghorn.

Rub two sandpaper blocks together in a long-short rhythm: CHUG-chug, CHUG-chug. Slowly pick up speed for the sound of a train.

Lightly bang the open ends of two shallow paper or plastic cups together. With practice, you will get the clip-clop sounds of a trotting horse. A galloping horse has a different rhythm that takes more practice to create. It's a quickly repeated da-da-<u>dum</u>, da-da-<u>dum</u>, da-da-<u>dum</u> . . .

Talk into a paper cup to imitate the sound of a voice on the telephone.

Put cornstarch in a large plastic bag so that it is half full. Close the bag tightly. Press the bag with your hands against a hard surface. Make sure you don't break the bag. Hear the crunch of your boot in the snow? Repeat the moves in a rhythm to sound like footsteps.

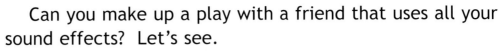

Can you make up a play with a friend that uses all your sound effects? Let's see.

**It was a dark and stormy night . . .**

47

# A BANGS AND TWANGS BAND
## WITH HUMS, SQUAWKS, AND TOOTS

You can get your friends together and make your own band. Here is a list of some of the instruments you can use:

spoon banging a pan
comb and tissue kazoo
rubber band stretched over the open top
    of a shoe box and twanged

two pencils used as drumsticks on Saran
    Wrap stretched over a cooking pot
walkie-talkie squawker
straw squeaker
paper, plastic, or tape whistle

Besides these instruments, you can invent your own. Add a singer or two, if you like. Your band may create sounds never heard before in the history of the world.